KNOWLEDGE MANAGEMENT AND LIBRARIES

An Annotated Bibliography 1997-2009

KNOWLEDGE MANAGEMENT AND LIBRARIES

An Annotated Bibliography 1997-2009

Lynette Lawrence Ralph

With a Foreword by
Timothy J. Ellis

The Edwin Mellen Press
Lewiston•Queenston•Lampeter

Library of Congress Cataloging-in-Publication Data

Ralph, Lynette Lawrence.
  Knowledge management and libraries : an annotated bibliography 1997-2009 / Lynette Lawrence Ralph ; with a foreword by Timothy [J.] Ellis.
    p. cm.
  Includes bibliographical references and index.
  ISBN-13: 978-0-7734-1298-9
  ISBN-10: 0-7734-1298-0
  I. Title.

                              2010021492

hors série.

A CIP catalog record for this book is available from the British Library.

Front cover: *Red and Green Reflections* © Frieda O. Weise, by permission of the photographer

          The Edwin Mellen Press   The Edwin Mellen Press
                Box 450   Box 67
          Lewiston, New York   Queenston, Ontario
          USA 14092-0450   CANADA L0S 1L0

                        The Edwin Mellen Press, Ltd.
                        Lampeter, Ceredigion, Wales
                        UNITED KINGDOM SA48 8LT

                  Printed in the United States of America

Dedication

Dedicated to Fari, Semai, and Sofia

Table of Contents

Foreword

One of the great joys of a teacher is to see a former student and protégé become a respected scholar and colleague. I feel very fortunate indeed to have witnessed and in a small way encouraged this transformation for Dr. Lynette Ralph, the author of this book.

This book represents months of hard work identifying, analyzing, synthesizing, and evaluating countless scholarly articles concerned with knowledge management, especially in respect to the potential to use the associated technologies and processes to improve the timeliness and accuracy of the reference librarian. The fruits of that exhaustive literature review formed the basis not only of a number of publications in respected conferences and scholarly journals.

The value of this compilation of annotated citations is undeniable. The breadth and depth of these reviews serve as an excellent starting point for the serious scholar interested in the knowledge management domain.

Timothy J. Ellis, Ph.D.

Professor

Graduate School of Computer and Information Sciences

Nova Southeastern University

3301 College Ave., FT Lauderdale-Davie, FL 33314-7796

Preface

This publication was conceived after completing several hours of research, which, focused on knowledge management and libraries. If it existed at the time of my research, I would have benefited from a publication such as this one. As an annotated bibliography of resources covering information on Knowledge Management and Libraries, this text could serve as an analytical tool that assists in-depth research and provides the unique information required by specialists in the area of knowledge management and libraries.

Scope and Purpose

A review of the literature demonstrates that bibliographies exist on knowledge management and so do a significant number of resources on libraries and knowledge management. However, there is no bibliography with a focus of knowledge management and libraries. While a bibliography is a traditional tool used to review, manage, and locate materials, an annotated bibliography is useful because it is more than a mere list of resources. Annotated bibliographies provide a way for others to decide whether a source will be helpful to their research. Annotated bibliographies also facilitate librarians in the identification of essential resources to fill subject gaps or even to strengthen certain subject areas in the collection. As Nosakhere, Hughes and Mosby (2004) observed, "Annotated bibliographies do not expire with time; they become more valuable as a 'resource of resources' with tracings for possible future acquisition" (p. xiii). Since knowledge management (KM) as a field emerged in the late 1990s, this publication will cover the period 1997-2009.

Content of Work

This book is designed for use as a text, a reference or a guide to the study of knowledge management and libraries. It is divided into three parts: journal articles, electronic resources, and books.

v

Acknowledgements

It is not possible to complete a work of this nature without the help and support of many people. I would first like to thank my dear friend Diane Johnson for her continued support and thorough understanding and application of APA style. I would also like to thank Lori Smith and Cathy Tijerino for their careful and intelligent reading and editing, my husband and sons for their support and encouragement, my library director, Eric Johnson, for his positive energies and encouragement, and finally my former director and friend, Frieda Weise for the use of her photographic skills. One of her photographs graces the cover of this book.

Lynette Ralph

Journal Articles

Abell, A. (2002). Fad or future. *Update, 1*(7), 30-32.

> In this article the author acknowledges the growth of knowledge management (KM) and suggests that KM has become so popular that it is now considered mainstream. He observes that although businesses have moved on to new concepts such as customer relationship management (CRM) and attention management, KM has become an embedded process that has evolved into working practices. The use of computers has enhanced the process of KM. Computers have aided in connecting people to people and the resources they need and allowed them to share information more effectively and in a more timely manner. The author also examines the characteristics of KM and the core competencies of KM leaders, and concludes that KM is more than just a fad. This article is useful because although it does not deal directly with libraries it accentuates the fact that KM is a useful tool for improving services in any type of institution.

Abram, S. (1997). Post information age positioning for special librarians: Is knowledge management the answer? *Information Outlook, 1*(6), 18-25.

> In attempting to answer the question of whether knowledge management (KM) is the answer to post information age positioning of special librarians, this article focuses on special librarianship as a profession and the Special Librarian Association. The author discusses creation and dissemination of information as an ability of the information business, operation of KM, building blocks of information, and knowledge environments. He sees all these issues as the key to successful

transformational librarianship. The author argues that Special Libraries are not fact-keepers but "catalysts in the knowledge continuum." This article is particularly interesting because it lists selected knowledge management websites.

Ajiferuke, I. (2003). Role of information professionals in knowledge management programs: Empirical evidence from Canada. *Informing Science Journal, 6,* 247-257.

In this study the author discusses the role of information professionals in knowledge management (KM) programs in Canada. Factors such as gender, age, and educational background (i.e. highest educational qualifications and discipline) did not seem to have any relationship with involvement in KM programs. Many of those involved in the programs played key roles, such as the design of the information architecture, development of taxonomy, or content management of the organization's intranet. Others played lesser roles, such as providing information for the intranet, gathering competitive intelligence, or providing research services as requested by the knowledge management team.

The research reveals that the implementation of a KM program in any organization has the potential of improving customer services, quickly bringing new products to market, and reducing cost of business operations. Information technologies are often used in KM programs in informing clients and employees of the latest innovation/development in the business sector as well as sharing knowledge among the employees.

Albert, J. (2000). Is knowledge management really the future for information professionals? In K. Srikantaiah & M. Koenig, (Eds). *Knowledge Management for the Information Professional,* pp. 63-76. Medford, NJ: Information Today.

In this chapter the author examines whether knowledge management (KM) is really the future for information professionals. The author points out that current management literature typically emphasize access to and organization of internal data. In this study, the roots and biases of major schools of KM are explored to see why this is so. The author describes the various ways that information specialists are most likely to encounter KM initiatives that do not begin with the information center. He also discusses the prospects of increased status for information professionals who adopt KM.

Balcombe, J. (1999). Getting out of the box: The role of the information professional in knowledge management. *The Law Librarian, 31*(2), 91-95.

In this article the author defines knowledge management (KM) as, "systematically sharing, using and creating knowledge to add value to the organization." The author believes that the practice of KM offers information professionals the opportunity to get out of the box of the library and information center and move into more strategic areas of the organization. The author makes the point that KM is not so much about managing knowledge as it is about managing people and changes and realizing that in order to successfully manage knowledge, the leaders have to create opportunity for changing the culture so that people will be more willing to share. For example, the policies and procedures should promote a positive learning environment that removes barriers to sharing and innovation. Job descriptions, internal communications, employee orientations, performance reviews, and even the exit interview should all promote the sharing of knowledge.

The author is Head of Information Science at The Industrial Society. She shares the view of the importance of improving culture with other corporate librarians. The article is useful because it focuses on the value of KM and specifically the value of KM in libraries.

Bang, T. (2004). Knowledge sharing in a learning resource center using a metro map metaphor for organizing web-based resources. *IFLA Publications, 108*, 169-183.

In this paper, the author describes a knowledge sharing project at the Aarhus School of Business (ASB) between the Faculty of Modern Languages and the Library. This cooperation resulted in the establishment of a Learning Resource Centre (LRC). Various innovative initiatives are described, especially within the development and the testing of new forms of communication and learning, and the integration of the information resources of the electronic research library. One example of a project described was the development of software for the sharing of knowledge - a "metro map" used for navigating the electronic information resources. This software was the result of an exchange of knowledge between professional departments at ASB and a software company.

The article is useful because it focuses on the importance of sharing knowledge of new trends and paradigm shifts in scholarly research methods and views knowledge sharing as an investment in future library services.

Bencivengo, G., Bambrick, J. & Nixon, C. (2003, May). *How librarians rank knowledge management.* Paper presented at the InfoToday Conference, Way Beyond Cool: Information for the Real World. New York, N.Y.

The authors acknowledge that since its first mention in the professional literature, knowledge management (KM) has taken information professionals by storm. Special librarians specifically have had a longstanding interest in the concept, and many articles discuss the definition and impact of KM within the world of online information. The authors then explore the particular appeal of KM to law librarians. Through a review of the professional literature they examine what has been published on law libraries and librarians in conjunction with KM and uncover additional Web-based resources. These authors investigate whether law librarians have pursued KM sufficiently or if there is need for further exploration. They report the results of this investigation, and discuss the use of KM in law firms.

Bhatt, G. D. (2001). Knowledge management in organizations: Examining the interaction between technologies, techniques and people. *Journal of Knowledge Management, 5*(1), 68-75.

This author argues that the knowledge management (KM) process can be categorized into knowledge creation, knowledge validation, knowledge presentation, knowledge distribution, and knowledge application activities. To capitalize on knowledge an organization must be swift in balancing its knowledge management activities. In general, such a balancing act requires changes in organizational culture, technologies, and techniques. A number of organizations believe that by focusing exclusively on people, technologies, or techniques, they can manage knowledge. However, that exclusive focus on people, technologies, or techniques does not enable a firm to sustain its competitive advantages. It is, rather, the interaction between technology, techniques, and people that allow an organization to manage its knowledge effectively. By creating a nurturing and "learning-by-doing" kind of environment, an organization can sustain its competitive advantages.

Additionally, knowledge creation refers to the ability to originate novel and useful ideas and solutions. As a result, when an organization knows what it knows, values and prioritizes that knowledge, and develops systems for leveraging and sharing and better decision-making, then it all leads directly to the creation of new knowledge.

Bizjak, P. (2005). Mankind's memory managers: A new paradigm of library science. *Library Philosophy and Practice, 2*(2), 1-10.

The author of this article considers the fundamental basis for library science and the proper course of study for librarians, in light of the complex array of information needs and the forms that information takes. The physical form of a carrier of information is considered together with the content of that physical item. The power of digital information is also considered.

According to the author, librarians hold and transfer the objectified memory of mankind. As a result, their task is to eliminate time-space limitations when transferring material by means of digitization and to index the material in such a way to enable users to find what they search for regardless of the criteria used. This article is useful because it demonstrates the significance of the relationship between library science and KM.

Blair, D. (2002). Knowledge management: Hype, hope, or help? *Journal of the American Society for Information Science and Technology, 53*(12), 1019-1028.

The author of this article provides insight into the difference between information management and knowledge management (KM). According to Blair, KM is not so much the management of tangible assets such as data or information, but the active management and support of expertise. The author emphasizes that expertise exists in people, and much of this kind of knowledge is tacit (or implicit) rather than explicit.

The author, a university professor of business, also discusses the distinction between tacit and explicit knowledge as another important concept in knowledge management. He focuses on five specific questions: what is knowledge; why are people, especially managers, thinking about KM; what are the enabling technologies for knowledge management; what are the prerequisites for KM; and what are the major challenges for KM? This article is important because it provides insight into the discussion of KM, and shows how information science relates to KM.

Branin, J.J. (2003). Knowledge management in academic libraries: Building the knowledge bank at the Ohio State University. *Journal of Library Administration, 39*(4), 41-56.

In this article the author traces the development of knowledge management (KM) in academic libraries. According to this author, collection development evolved to collection management, then to KM. The author points out that budget constraints forced librarians to move from indiscriminately developing a collection to managing the collection. Later as technology contributed to overwhelming resources, the focus became the management of knowledge. The author, who at the time was

Director of Libraries at Ohio State, discusses his library's attempt to manage knowledge by developing a knowledge bank project.

The author recognizes the importance of KM. The article traces the history and development of KM, and also discusses the importance of capturing tacit knowledge, while sharing explicit knowledge. It underscores the point that in order for librarians to effectively meet the needs of students and faculty, they must extend their expertise beyond collection management to KM.

Branin, J. (2009, March). What we need is a knowledge management perspective. *College and Research Libraries, 70*(2), 104-105.

In this article, the author discusses the importance of knowledge management (KM) in academic librarianship. The author believes that the responsibilities of academic librarians extend beyond the collection and development of the libraries' scholarly resources. These librarians need to be able to effectively navigate the digital resources available in academic libraries. The author discusses how digital media has impacted the library service model. This article is significant because the author effectively portrays the significance of KM as a useful aspect of academic librarianship.

Broadbent, M. (1998). The phenomenon of knowledge management: What does it mean to the   information profession? *Information Outlook*, 2(5), 23-36.

In this article the author explores the phenomenon of knowledge management (KM) and its role for the information professional. The author who is a professional librarian with a background in academic management, indicates that KM is about enhancing the use of organizational knowledge through sound practices of information management and organizational learning. The main purpose of KM, she feels, is to deliver value to the organization. According to the author KM is not owned by any one group in any organization, nor by any one profession or industry. Librarians, she opines are highly motivated to provide access to information as well as share information. However, if they want to be successful in KM they need to understand the varying perspectives of the other participants. The author concludes that KM requires a holistic and multidisciplinary approach to management processes and an understanding of the dimensions of knowledge work.

Brogan, M., Hingston, P. et al. (2001, August). *A bounded or unbounded universe? Knowledge management in postgraduate LIS education*. Paper presented at the 67th annual IFLA council and general conference, Boston, MA.

In this paper the authors investigate the unique contribution knowledge management (KM) could make to a library and information science (LIS) education, and the role an LIS education could play in enhancing the value of KM. To answer these questions, the authors conducted a study and reported on the research and consultative processes. The population sampled, were practitioners in the library, information management, records management, and computing industry sector fields in Australia. A survey instrument was designed to measure preferences in terms of course content and course options; industry demand for KM qualified personnel, and attitudes toward KM. A Likert scale was used to determine how respondents perceived KM. Statements focused on three key dimensions of attitude toward KM: denoting expectations, identification or belonging, and perceived valued. Respondents were invited to say whether they: regarded KM as durable; saw themselves as Knowledge Managers; and could see career benefits in learning more about KM. Data are presented for sample population characteristics, KM training needs (course content), course options, employability, and attitudes toward KM. A provisional postgraduate studies model for a KM course is described.

The results show that participants believe that KM is multidisciplinary with a positive future. It is not an unbounded universe, but is on an evolutionary path in which LIS professionals can play a significant role.

Chaudhry, A. S., & Higgins, S. (2003). On the need for a multidisciplinary approach to education for knowledge management. *Library Review, 52*(1/2): 65-70.

In this paper the authors report the findings of a study of knowledge management (KM) courses included in the curriculum of academic disciplines of business, computing and information. Based on a review of course descriptions selected from web sites of universities in different countries, the authors describe levels of courses, curriculum areas and topics, and differences in emphasis in teaching knowledge management courses in different departments and schools. They highlight the multidisciplinary nature of the curriculum and suggest a collaborative approach in designing and conducting balanced KM education programs.

Chaudhry, A. S. & Higgins, S. (2004). Education for knowledge management: A spectrum approach. *IFLA Publications, 108*, 127-136.

The authors in this chapter report the findings of a study of knowledge management (KM) courses included in the curriculum of academic disciplines of business, computing, and information studies. Based on a review of course descriptions selected from web sites of universities in different countries, the authors describe levels of courses, curriculum areas and topics, and differences in emphasis in teaching knowledge management courses in different departments and schools.

The authors highlight the multi-disciplinary nature of the curriculum and suggested a collaborative approach in designing and conducting KM education programs. Institutions of higher education tend to encourage the type of research culture most appropriate to the learning the university wants to encourage in its students. Practice-based institutions seek to focus on practice-based education and practice-based, or context-driven research. Such communities build on the history and culture of the higher education system that has evolved in each country. A thorough understanding both of the traditional print basis of librarianship and electronic means of collecting, organizing and disseminating information is needed for a multidimensional approach to understanding and working with KM.

Cheng, G. (2001). The shifting information landscape: Reinventing the wheel or a whole new frontier for librarians. *New Library World, 102*(1160/1161), 26-33.

This author focuses on the explosive growth and overwhelming use of Web resources and observed that this growth has fuelled the misconception that the library is no longer relevant and one can find any information on the web. She discusses the various roles of librarians including developing competent health care professionals. She draws a parallel analogy from knowledge management literature, and highlights the importance of adding value to the process of transforming data to information, and from information to knowledge. Cheng maintains that by participating in knowledge building and application in the local environment, the new roles in publishing, marketing, teaching, researching, collaborating, and building up the knowledge base emerged, demonstrating that the traditional role of a library as being a repository and providers of information is no longer adequate. The author proposes that continuous education and training in new skills will better equip librarians for these new roles, and at the same time, preserve the traditional and professional value of providing quality information to those in need.

Clarke, R. (2004). Knowledge management in the main library, the University of the West Indies, Trinidad. *Information Development, 20*(1), 30-34.

In this article the author proposes that in order for knowledge management (KM) to be successful in any organization there must be a navigational tool. In the authors' institution, University of the West Indies (U.W.I.) Trinidad, this tool is the *Secretariat Manual*. This manual maintains the records of the administration and various sections. It consists of over 200 pages of detailed instruction and includes samples of forms, memos and letters. The Secretariat Manual captures both tacit and explicit knowledge. As a result it aides the library in finding, selecting, organizing, disseminating, and transferring important information and expertise necessary for problem-solving, strategic planning, and decision-making. This article underscores the importance of KM and points out the necessity of having a knowledge management tool that captured the knowledge of the library thus allowing it to be used and shared by others in the future.

Corrall, S. (1998/1999). Are we in the knowledge management business? *Ariadne*, (18), 16-18.

In this article the author considers the question of whether academic libraries are in the business of knowledge management (KM). He observes that due to the complicated nature of knowledge per se and its consequent management, it is often difficult to estimate or demonstrate the value of knowledge management. As a result, academic libraries, with limited budget and human resources, often hesitate to follow the business sector and plunge into the uncharted sea of KM. This paper suggests a pragmatic approach to the implementation of KM for academic libraries: utilizing the existing staffing, technology, and management structure. This article is useful because it clearly delineated an approach for the incorporation of KM into academic libraries.

14

Davenport, E. (2004). Organizations, knowledge management and libraries: Issues, opportunities and challenges. *IFLA Publications, 108*, 81-89

      The author in this paper suggests that both special and industrial libraries and their organizations currently face transformation because of a combination of societal, economic and technological factors. As a result of new structures and work patterns, four challenges have been introduced – context, codification, customization and collaboration. She discusses these challenges in terms of the four quadrants of Nonaka's "knowledge spiral" model. She suggests that for knowledge management to be effective in libraries, librarians must move beyond their traditional niche.

Davenport, E., & Cronin, B. (2000). Knowledge management: Semantic drift or conceptual shift. *Journal of Education for Library and Information Science, 41*(4), 294-306.

      This paper offers an exploration of knowledge management (KM), a concept the authors felt was only partially understood in domains that use the term. Three such domains are described: library and information science (LIS), business administration, and organization theory. In the case of LIS, KM is predominantly seen as information management by another name (semantic drift); in the case of business administration, it appears to be brought on board as an antidote to excessive focus on process at the expense of human expertise; the third aspect organization theory articulates a major conceptual shift, presenting organizations as adaptive entities that co-evolve with a given environment.

      According to the authors, LIS and business administration may be distinguished by an over-emphasis on codification and myopia with regard to human expertise, tacit knowledge, social learning, trust, and intuition.

Business administration and organization theory (in contrast to LIS) focuses on the internal as much as the external (reflexivity) and on the critical importance of relationships and exchange (reciprocity). The authors suggest that tensions may arise in any organization committed to KM where different domains have different understandings because KM is a complex and multidimensional concept that requires diverse insights. This article is interesting because it assesses, analyzes and contrasts the similarities and differences of LIS, business administration and organization theory and how it relates to KM.

Davenport, T. H., & Prusak, L. (2004). Prelude: Blow up the corporate library. *IFLA Publications, 108*, 11-19.

In this article the authors examine why many corporate libraries play only a marginal role in today's corporation. According to the authors, librarians are uniquely equipped to play significant roles in the current information –intensive environment, and some of them do. Yet in many cases, these corporate libraries do not get the credit or financial support they deserve. In order to change this, the authors recommend that the corporate library should be blown up and radical changes implemented, creating a new model. This new model would expand the mission, function and scope of the library and recognize the true value and worth of the librarian as an information specialist who understands what information is needed and how to facilitate the effective delivery of that information. This article is interesting because it demonstrates the role KM can play in the effective delivery of information.

16

Dillon, M. (1999). Knowledge management opportunities for libraries and
universities. *The Library and Information Science Annual, 7*, 3-11.

In this article the author discusses various knowledge management
(KM) opportunities for libraries and universities. Dillon points-out that
KM is not new and credits Peter Drucker for having the insight to
recognize that the knowledge revolution would create an upsurge in the
availability and access of information, thus requiring a management of
knowledge.

The author who is the Director of OCLC Institute describes KM as
a basis for decision-making and increasing efficiency in any university or
library. According to Dillon, if universities and libraries are systematic in
exploiting knowledge it will improve their services. KM can also be
effective in libraries and universities because of the expertise that exists in
these areas. Various professors and librarians possess various types of
degrees. This can allow for the developing of an expertise database that
captures the skills, background and work experience of the staff. This
database should conveniently be available and contain the information that
would allow anyone in the institution to identify, "an individual staff
person with a specific capability when the need for such a capability
arises." If such a database exists it would capture explicit as well as tacit
knowledge.

The author also discusses the contributions that libraries could
make to KM on the campus. He cites four examples for which librarians
could take leadership. These include designing and maintaining the
university's website, creating and maintaining an online inventory of
university-supported knowledge assets, establishing enters for dealing
with online access to university knowledge assets, and serving as KM
consultants.

DiMattia, S., & Oder, N. (1997). Knowledge management: Hope, hype or harbinger? *Library Journal, 2*(2): 321-326.

In this article the authors examine the emergence of knowledge management (KM), business world variations on its concepts, the role of and opportunities for librarians, and professional competencies. KM, the author believes, rose out of organizational downsizing and technology innovation and was an attempt to cope with the information explosion and to capitalize on increased knowledge in the workplace. Several librarians are interviewed and their opinions of KM are represented. These librarians discuss the important and evolving role of librarians in the area of KM and the need for flexibility. This article focuses on special libraries.

Duffy, J. (2000). Knowledge management: What every information professional should know. *The Information Management Journal, 34*(3): 10-18.

In this article the author identifies what every information manager needs to appreciate fully the scope and opportunity that knowledge management (KM) offered to the extended enterprise. It examined how to maximize the potential of organizational knowledge, how to use KM to out-think the competition, and the difference between knowledge and information.

New Web-enabled technologies continue to expand the reach of the extended enterprise. This expansion demands new and more complex skills of all information management and information technology professionals to facilitate its evolution. As the global reach of business expands and companies become larger and more geographically dispersed, it becomes increasingly difficult for them to know where their best

knowledge is and even more difficult for them to "know what they know."
This article will help information professionals and others to recognize
and exploit the full potential of organizational knowledge. Because every
employee can potentially contribute to enhancing an organization's
knowledge, the information here is intended for widespread distribution.

Fergurson, S. (2004, September). *The knowledge management myth: Will the real
knowledge managers please step forward?* Paper presented at ALIA
Biennial Conference, Queensland, Australia.

In this article the author focuses on the issue of what library and
information professionals had to contribute to knowledge management.
From the author's perspective, librarians are not knowledge workers
capable of taking over the knowledge management functions of their
organizations. Instead he sees the role of the librarian as distinct from that
of a knowledge worker. From his perspective, the librarian is an
information manager who could work closely with a knowledge worker
but not replace one.

This author contradicts several authors, Branin (2003) and Dillon
1999) who feel that librarians, like knowledge workers demonstrate skills
and expertise and are also perceived as experts by their institutions.

Fisher, A. (1998). So what is the big fuss about? *La record, 100*(4), 190-191.

In this article, the author defines knowledge management (KM) and discusses its value to organizations. According to the author, "the more efficient an organization is in using KM, the greater its opportunity to improve performance." The author discusses the role knowledge management had traditionally played in businesses and points out that KM had for some time been around in libraries, especially the special libraries, since these libraries were often attached to businesses. However the author feels that with time special librarians will position themselves to take advantage of KM as a tool.

The author, who is a policy adviser at the Library and Information Commission, emphasizes the value of KM in libraries, seeing it as an essential part of the librarians' "portfolio of skills." This article validates the value of KM as a tool that could create greater efficiency in libraries.

Gandhi, S. (2004). Knowledge management and reference services. *The Journal of Academic Librarianship, 30*(5), 368-381.

In this article, the author discusses the value of knowledge management (KM) as a means to capture the intellectual capital of employees. The article defines the key concepts of KM and reviews various KM initiatives. The author made the observation that for KM to be effective, it is essential to capture both tacit and explicit knowledge. Finally, the author discusses KM and its relevance for reference work in libraries. According to the author, KM could be divided into two parts. The first is the management of data and information, while the second is the management of individuals who possess specific expertise, abilities or knowledge.

In discussing the role of KM in reference services, the author cites research to show that because of the overwhelming amount of information to which they were exposed, no single librarian can keep track of or remember the best sources of information. As a result, reference librarians manage to answer only 50-60% of questions correctly. The author concluded that KM systems were needed to tap into the communal knowledge of librarians.

Ghani, S. R. (2009). Knowledge management: Tools and techniques. *Journal of Library & Information Technology, 29*(6), 33-38.

In this paper, the author points-out that knowledge management (KM) is not one single discipline, but an integration of numerous endeavors and fields of study. He provides a framework for characterizing the various tools and techniques available to KM practitioners, and an overview of a number of key terms and concepts. Additionally, he describes the framework, provides examples of how to use it, and explores a variety of potential application areas. The stress of KM tools and techniques, the author said, has been maneuvered to share knowledge through communication and collaboration tools, which specify the shift from process to practice.

Hayes, H. (2004). The role of libraries in the knowledge economy. *Serials: The Journal for the Serials Community, 17*(3): 231- 238. doi: 10.1629/17231.

In this paper, the author examines the role of libraries in the knowledge economy. She points out that the knowledge economy and the growth of knowledge management (KM), is an essential competency of organizations and provides new opportunities for librarians and information specialists to expand existing roles and utilize the skills they have honed to meet corporate objectives. The key information management role of both internal and external information, combined with the contribution to information competence and the ability to contextualize information, contributes to organizational excellence, customer benefit and competitive advantage which can be achieved more effectively through collaboration and partnership.

Hazeri, A., Sarrafzadeh, M., & Martin, B. (2007). Reflections of information professionals on knowledge management: Competencies in the LIS curriculum. *Journal of Education for Library & Information Science, 48*(3), 168-186.

In this paper, the author presents a range of professional perspectives on the competencies required for the practice of knowledge management (KM) by library and information science (LIS) professionals and the strength of current curricula in this area. He accomplishes this by drawing on the findings of two research projects, and on earlier studies. His research reveals that KM has provided LIS professionals with a wide variety of new career opportunities. As a multi-dimensional discipline KM requires an expanded breadth of knowledge with a mix of different skills. Considerable efforts have been made to compile KM competency profiles for LIS based on an analysis of market needs and on the perspectives of the many groups involved. This article is interesting because it examines the LIS curriculum that offered KM and discusses the role KM played in the knowledge base and competence of these professionals.

Hazeri, A., Martin, B., & Sarrafzadeh, M. (2009). Integration of knowledge management with the library and information science curriculum: Some professional perspectives. *Journal of Education for Library and Information Science, 50*(3), 152-163.

In this paper the authors examine the focus of current Library and Information Science (LIS) curricula in addressing knowledge management (KM) and related concepts. The authors share that this growing recognition of the importance of KM led to calls for curriculum review in LIS and resulted in a research project on the implications of KM for LIS education. This issue was investigated from the viewpoint of the LIS community. The methodology consisted of both a web- based survey and in-depth interviews with 18 LIS heads of schools or senior staff at schools operating KM programs and courses. The findings indicate that there is considerable interest within the LIS community in expanding their curricula to include a stronger element of KM. Notable benefits are the potential broadening of professional perspectives to wider areas and enhancement of the image of LIS professionals both within and outside the profession. Additionally, it includes the intensive coverage of knowledge in all its forms and the inclusion of more organizational, business and management issues in the curriculum along with an emphasis on the practical dimensions of knowledge management.

Hazeri, A., Martin, B., & Sarrafzadeh, M. (2009). Exploring the benefits of KM education for LIS professionals. *Education for Information 27*(1), 1-20.

This paper is a follow up to a research study completed in 2008 on the implications of knowledge management (KM) for library and information science (LIS) education. It is to be expected that in a new and emerging discipline like KM there still will be ambivalence among both LIS educational institutions and their students as to the need to have KM courses. The author feels that investigating the benefits of engaging with these programs might help to clear up this ambiguity. The previous research sought perceptions of the LIS international community and in particular LIS academics. From the findings it became clear that the LIS community has a positive view of the potential outcomes of KM education for LIS students. Participants in the current research also acknowledge the cultivation of additional competencies among KM learners, as a contribution to the improved professionalism of corporate librarians, and the provision of new career options for LIS graduates. This article is interesting because it is a follow-up of a previously conducted study.

Hazeri, A & Martin, B. (2009). Responding to the challenges of KM education in the LIS sector: some academic and professional perspectives. *Australian Library Journal,58*(3), 250-268.

In this paper the authors present the follow-up findings of recent research into the challenges of knowledge management (KM) education in the field of library and information science (LIS). The initial research was in the form of an online survey canvassing the views of the wider LIS community on the responsibility of LIS schools for KM education; the second consisted of a collection of in-depth interviews with LIS academics who were engaged in education for KM. It is clear that the main challenges associated with KM education in the LIS discipline concern people's perceptions of KM and the place of KM in LIS education, Changes need to be made, both to these perceptions and to the ways in which LIS schools market and package their KM offerings. As a newly emerging field of study, KM education is faced with significant challenges which continue to evolve. Informed by wider organizational perspectives,

Jain, P. (2009). Knowledge management for 21st century information professionals. *Journal of Knowledge Management Practice, 10*(2).

In this article, the author discusses the importance of knowledge management (KM) for 21st century information professionals; their evolving new roles, skills and challenges. Jain observes that library science has been incessantly evolving due to the rapidly changing information and communication technology (ICT). He points out that the internet has further transformed the information society into to a global society. Thus the knowledge explosion and ICT tools have equipped information and library science with immediate access to practically limitless sources, plus quick storage, retrieval and sharing tools. In this knowledge economy age information professionals' roles have therefore changed profoundly at both library practitioner and library school educator levels. On the library side information professionals have evolved from traditional cataloguer and research and reference service providers to value added service providers, teacher librarians and, most recently, knowledge managers. On the library school educators' side, there is the constant challenge to review the curriculum, keep up to date and extend personal capacity according to the needs of the knowledge society.

In this paper the author not only looks specifically at the significance and challenges of KM for 21st century information professionals but he also recommends important issues to have in place for information professionals to be a successful partner of this KM economy.

Jain, P. & Mutula, S. (2008). Libraries as learning organisations: Implications for knowledge management. *Library HiTech News, 25*(8), 10.

In this paper the authors describe how libraries are under increasing pressure to become learning organizations for better knowledge management (KM) and to cultivate a culture of continuing learning to cope with both current and future changes in their organizations. The authors point out that currently libraries have a central place and integral role in higher education. However, as higher education evolves, the library and librarians have to also evolve to be compatible with the changing times and technology and thus be perceived as a learning organization. Thus to successfully become a learning organization, libraries must create the climate for change and innovation. Jain and Mutula believe that libraries should create learning environments by working collaboratively with other disciplines, especially educators and community developers. These libraries should also be better equipped to cope with independent learning, should be flexible and finally it is important for libraries to promote a culture of knowledge sharing and collective learning.

Jantz, R. (2001). Knowledge management in academic libraries: Special tools and processes to support information professionals. *Reference Services Review, 29*(1), 33-39.

In this article the author discusses a knowledge management (KM) tool that was developed by a team of reference librarians from different libraries within the New Brunswick Campus of Rutgers University. This tool was developed because the librarians felt the need to interact more fully with the librarians on the various campuses and also to utilize their varying backgrounds and expertise, by sharing information. This article examines the importance of KM within academic libraries and discusses how reference librarians could be more effective if they utilized a tool that facilitated KM.

Joyline, M. (2008). Knowledge management and international organizations: Perspectives on information professionals' role. *Libri: International Journal of Libraries and Information Services, 58*(3), 144-154.

This study explains the importance of including an information professional in all the systematic processes of knowledge management (KM). According to the author, the rapid evolution of information and communication technology in recent years has seen KM become a key tool for the success of a variety of institutions. Many international organizations have developed KM programs as key to their future development strategies. The number of international organizations that have identified KM as one of their core management tools or formed a new knowledge management department is growing every day. Thus, the International Federation of Red Cross and Red Crescent Societies (IFRC), International Labor Office (ILO), United Nations and International

Monetary Fund (IMF) have now created KM divisions within their structures. Yet despite its growing popularity, KM in international organizations remains a complex and challenging task. It calls for the management and integration of knowledge bases across national boundaries, in diverse cultural settings, and within organizations that may possess distinct values and sets of priorities.

Using the case study method, the author examines the IFRC and identifies the roles through which the librarians' professional training can be leveraged for knowledge capturing, organization, and dissemination in an organization such as the IFRC.

Kaufman, D. (2002). Turning search into knowledge management. *The Electronic Library, 20*(1), 49-54.

In this article the author discusses the process of changing data into an effective knowledge management (KM) system. According to the author computers cannot be relied upon to understand concepts and context within which information is provided. The author suggests similarity ranking as an effective mechanical process of organizing data. He gives examples of how a search done by a search engine could provide information that was completely irrelevant. One example given is searching for information on the "eating disorders of men." This search provided a document on "Boyz II Men," a musical group. The author discusses that similarity ranking is essential to KM systems and without this a high quality system could not exist. This article is useful because it underscores the importance of creating or acquiring a KM product that was effective.

Keeling, C., & Hornby, S. (1999). Knowledge management in the networked public library. *Managing Information, 6*(8): 27-29.

The author observes that knowledge management (KM) is becoming popular in institutional libraries, specifically in those organizations who utilize their intellectual capital. Additionally, the library and information science (LIS) community has begun to promote the use of KM and encourage librarians across all sectors to apply its principles where appropriate, or risk being marginalized by other, more efficient and flexible organizations who offer knowledge service. He discusses the impending delivery of the New Library Network to public libraries in the U.K. and concludes that application of KM principles and complimentary management structures can help public libraries establish their roles in the environment of the learning organization.

Khaiser, N. (2007). The changing role of a librarian in knowledge management environment. *SRELS Journal of Information Management, 44*(1): 15-26.

In this paper, the author examines the evolving role of librarians in the knowledge management (KM) environment. According to the author, we currently live in the Information Knowledge Era (IKE), which is changing rapidly. As a result, knowledge and information are the most vital resources for the growth and development of both individuals and organizations. These resources are assets, which are available in the form of databases, knowledge bases, and in the minds of people and organizations. Often work is duplicated, simply because co-workers are not aware of what is going on in other parts of the organization. Effectively utilizing KM could alleviate this problem. Librarians are currently facing many challenges, but those who recognize this change and willingly shift from the conventional role to the use of KM can be more successful and provide better quality service to their patrons.

Kim, S. (2000). The roles of knowledge professionals for knowledge management. *Inspel, 34*(1), 1-8.

In this paper the author discusses the concept of knowledge and its relationship to knowledge management (KM). The author divides knowledge into two types, tacit knowledge and explicit knowledge. He discusses both, then looks at the relationship of these two types of knowledge to KM. He feels that the significance of KM is to deliver value to the organization and affirm that both types of knowledge are necessary to do so.

The author then examines the roles of librarians as knowledge professionals and assesses their roles for achieving organizational goals. According to the author, librarians need to work as knowledge workers by demonstrating their skill and expertise and not being limited to being the custodians or keepers of information. He feels that the librarian as a knowledge professional should move from the background to the center of the organizational stage working closely with the users and technology experts, collecting and analyzing strategic intelligence, and also acting as the trainers and consultants "who transfer knowledge gathering and research skills throughout the organization." Like Aster and Choo (1995), this author feels that the basic goal of KM is to harness knowledge resources and capabilities of the organization so that it allowed them to learn and adapt to its changing environment.

This article is useful because it describes the notion of knowledge and KM and investigates the roles of librarians as knowledge professionals for achieving organizational goals. She admits that we are currently in an information and knowledge age and that knowledge is the most important factor for the long term success of any organization. She asserts that knowledge resides in "many different places such as databases, knowledge bases, filing cabinets, and people's heads."

30

Koenig, M. E. (2001). Knowledge management, user education and librarianship. *IFLA Publications, 108,* 137-150.

In this article, the author discusses the role of librarians in knowledge management (KM). He points out that librarians perform KM duties, some of which are obvious and some of which are not. The tasks of designing information systems, creating classification systems and taxonomies, and implementing and operating those systems are obvious. On the other hand, the tasks of librarians functioning in user education and training are not so obvious. Librarians are skilled in user education and training which they have traditionally called "bibliographic instruction." He also discusses the importance of rich communications, browsing, serendipity, and the phenomenon that information workers, from researchers to managers, tend to spend a surprisingly consistent 20%-25% of their work time in information seeking. He concludes that librarians have the potential to play a significant role in the areas of user education and training in the context of KM initiatives.

Koenig, M. (2005). KM moves beyond the organization: The opportunity for librarians. *Information Services & Use, 25* (2): 87-93.

In this article the author states that knowledge management (KM) is no ordinary management fad because it has longevity. The KM movement, the author points out, has gone through a number of stages and it is now moving into a stage of recognizing the importance of, and incorporating, information and knowledge external into the parent organization. He also observes that KM is relevant to and overlaps greatly with librarianship. Despite this obvious overlap with librarianship however, librarians have done very little in capitalizing on that overlap.

Koenig observes that incorporating information and knowledge sharing has always been the province of the librarian and the information professional. Thus the development and use of KM present obvious and important opportunities for the field of librarianship, particularly in the area of the organization's KM system design.

Koina, C. (2003). Librarians are the ultimate knowledge managers? *The Australian Library Journal, 52*(3): 269-272.

In this article the author ponders the question, are librarians the ultimate managers. Koina begins by defining knowledge management (KM) and identifying the skills essential to be an effective knowledge manager. The skills listed include flexibility, team work, people and communication skills, ability to assess and evaluate information, ability to create, record and store information effectively, ability to train and educate the client, and the ability to be client-oriented. According to Koina, librarians possess these skill sets, although they do not always demonstrate that they do. Next, the author points out that in addition to these skills, the image is of the knowledge manager is also important; knowledge managers must possess a certain image.

The current image of librarians Koina believes, is that they focus on acquisition or distribution of information acquired external to the organization. Records managers on the other hand, focus on documents internal or integral to its management. In such a situation no one group has an understanding of the overall information. Librarians then have several options, they could maintain the status quo and do nothing at all, or they could acquire the necessary skills and find ways to promote themselves and let their superiors be aware that they do possess the skills. They should not be afraid to brag, it is important that they find a balance and play to their strengths. If librarians demonstrate their skills and abilities and participate in self-promotion, it would become obvious that they are indeed the ultimate knowledge managers.

Lamont, J. (2004, January). Knowledge management at your service: New solutions and sources for librarians. *Searcher: The Magazine for Database Professionals, 12*(1), 57-61.

In this article the author observes that librarians have been associated with knowledge management (KM) for many years because they have always managed the collection and distribution of critical information based on knowing the information their clients need and the relevant sources required to meet those needs. The author, a research analyst at Zentek Corporation, points out that currently new software tools exist that could help the librarians be more effective in their traditional functions, while at the same time allowing them new opportunities to use their expertise behind the scenes. She also discusses additional tools that could enhance services. These include expertise in location and management (ELM) research retrieval software, and Business Intelligence (BI) software. This article is interesting because it acknowledges the use of knowledge management by librarians.

Lee, H. (2005). Knowledge management and the role of libraries. *Chinese Librarianship, 6*(19).

     In this article the author states that the development of knowledge management (KM) in recent years has become the key concern for librarians and libraries. This paper reviews the development of KM and compares the differences between information and knowledge as well as between information management and KM. It also examines the role of librarians/libraries in KM and suggests that librarians/libraries in the digital and knowledge age should be in charge of KM in their respective organizations in order to leverage the intellectual assets and facilitate knowledge creation.

Ling-Ling, L. (2005). Educating knowledge professionals in library and information science schools. *Journal of Educational Media & Library Sciences, 42*(3), 347- 362.

     In this paper the author acknowledges that knowledge management (KM) is a multidisciplinary subject area involving professionals with diverse backgrounds and investigates the required educational background and skills for KM professionals. Specifically, the focus of the paper is to examine whether a master's degree in library and information science (LIS) is a preferred educational background listed in KM-related job postings. In addition, the preferred skills and knowledge required by KM employers are analyzed to reveal the association with graduate courses in library and information science. Job postings were collected from various sources during a specific timeframe. Content analysis was used to discover the kinds of backgrounds, skills, and knowledge that are expected by the employers. By examining both KM literature and the job postings, the author concludes that a certain set of skills can be taught and essential knowledge can be obtained through the LIS curriculum.

Loughridge, B. (1999). Knowledge management, librarians and information managers: Fad or future? *New Library World, 100*(6), 245-253. doi: 10.1108/03074809910290486.

In this article, the author questions whether knowledge management (KM) is merely a fad or truly represents a significant shift in the future for librarians and information managers. To support his discussion, Loughridge reviews some recent professional and academic publications on aspects of the theory and practice of KM, with particular reference to the curriculum of professional education for library and information management. Some authors of those professional publications dismiss KM as a fad, while others view it as a major paradigm shift in the management and exploitation of "intellectual capital." After a thorough review, Loughridge concludes that many aspects of KM practice bear a close resemblance to well-established practices in librarianship and information management. However, the emphasis by KM theorists and practitioners on the importance of knowledge elicitation and knowledge creation, group work and team work, greater involvement in organizational strategy development and support and IT may require greater attention to the personality, motivation, and career aspirations of potential entrants to the profession in order to prepare them better for wider-ranging, multi-role careers.

Malhan, I. V., & Rao, S. (2005). From library management to knowledge management: A conceptual change. *Journal of Information & Knowledge Management. 4*(4), 269-277.

This is an opinion paper in which the author briefly outlines the nature and significance of conceptual changes involved in the practices of library management to its transition to knowledge management (KM). In this paper the author also discusses the competencies necessary for managing knowledge resources. According to the author, in the knowledge economy era, the library plays a very crucial role in the further extension and modification of knowledge. The growing need for KM has influenced every component and operation of a library. KM requires more effective methods of information handling, speedy transfer of information and linking of information with individuals and their activities. It demands library patron centered development of information systems and services and customization of information at the individual level.

Martin, B., Hazeri, A., & Sarrafzadeh, M. (2006). Knowledge management and the LIS professions: Investigating the implications for practice and for educational provision. *Australian Library Journal, 55*(1), 12-29.

In this paper the authors examine the complex web of interrelationships that is emerging as the library and information professions come to terms with the growing phenomenon of knowledge management (KM). This phenomenon manifests itself at one level in the wider organizational and business context, and at another in the professional and employment spheres. At the time of writing, two of the authors were doctoral students at RMIT University researching the issues arising from the developing relationship between the library and information professions and the KM phenomenon. This includes the potential threats and opportunities, the synergies and the potential for radically new visions and responses. In this paper the authors set these developments in the context of the new knowledge-based economy, the subsequent emergence of knowledge management, and its implications for the library and information professions as manifested both in professional practice and in educational preparation for such practice.

Matthews, R., & Nixon, C. (2002, March). *KM is not about technology: Strategies for librarians providing organization-wide context for capturing knowledge--as tested in a law firm.* Paper presented at the 17th Annual Computers in Libraries Conference. Washington, D.C.

The author discusses how knowledge management (KM) can be advanced by library professionals' special skills and uses a law firm to demonstrate this. The author states that unless a KM initiative is championed by the upper management of the parent organization, librarians should heed the technology component of KM. He describes how technology and KM are linked in law firms, with the vital components being practice management systems and an intranet designed to streamline the delivery of client services. He points out that technology is a starting point for building knowledge-sharing communities and that librarians are naturals in shaping this technology and its use. He explains in great detail the contributions of librarians in making practice management systems into knowledge-sharing communities. Finally, he provides blueprints for an effective intranet and gives examples of documents and other forms of captured knowledge. This article is useful because the author delineated the important steps for an effective KM system, and also discusses the significance of promotion and training tools.

Milne, P. (1999). Knowledge management and LIS education. *Education for Library & Information Services: Australia, 16*(3), 31-38.

In this article the author observes that library practice has changed dramatically over recent years, yet the perception is that librarians are essentially still doing what they have always done. She points out that only the tools have changed, but service to clients remains the core professional ethic. According to the author, in some circles it is the belief that the strong service ethic may be a handicap within knowledge-aware organizations. She examines the core findings of research which analyzes the role of information professionals within such organizations. Within the context of library and information science (*LIS*) education, she discusses the knowledge skills and attributes that are considered desirable for knowledge workers, and suggests methods for incorporating these into the LIS curriculum.

Morris, A. (2004). Knowledge management: Employment opportunities for IS graduates *IFLA Publications, 108,* 115-125.

In this paper the author presents the results of market research that was undertaken in preparation for a new postgraduate program in information and knowledge management (KM) at the Department of Information Science, Loughborough University. The research was needed to shape the curriculum and to define program parameters. The study investigates the availability and types of jobs in this field, the skills and types of personnel sought by employers, and whether demand is currently being met in the UK. The study involves identifying and analyzing national advertisements for knowledge managers over a six-month period and undertaking follow-up surveys involving the agencies and employers

38

who placed the advertisements. The author concludes undoubtedly new programs in Information and KM will open up considerable new employment opportunities for IS (Information Science) graduates.

Mphidi, H. (2004). The utilization of an intranet as a knowledge management tool in academic libraries. *Electronic Library, 22*(5), 393-400.

In this article the author states that the intranet has emerged as one of today's most effective tools for knowledge management (KM). This article reports on the extent to which three South African academic libraries, selected by means of the purposive sampling method, utilize the intranet as a KM tool. Based on the literature, KM and an intranet are briefly defined. The advantages of the intranet as a KM tool as well as the content of an intranet are discussed. The opinions about KM and the utilization of the intranet as a KM tool in the three academic libraries are weighed up against the findings in the literature. It is clear that a strong awareness exists of the importance of KM and the value of the intranet as a KM tool. However, the potential of the intranet as a KM tool is not utilized fully.

Nelson, E. (2008). Knowledge management for libraries. *Library Administration & Management, 22*(3): 135-137.

In this article the author discusses various forms of knowledge management (KM) tools and techniques as it pertains to librarians and a library setting. One technique discussed is Communities of Practice which are self-organized groups initiated by employees who communicate with each other because of their shared work practices, interests, or aims. Another technique and how it applies to knowledge management is Peer

Mentoring developed by Trautman of Microsoft. According to the author, Trautman believes that the knowledge of the mentor can be segmented so that the apprentice can assimilate information better and faster on a task-specific basis. Other knowledge management tools discussed are web 2.0, wikis and the tagging classification system.

Nitse, P.S., & Parker, K. R. (2002/2003). Library Science, knowledge management, competitive intelligence: Archive theory- the common link. *The Reference Librarian,* 79/80, 395-407.

The authors of this paper suggest that there is a common link among three disciplines, library science, knowledge management (KM), and competitive intelligence (CI). At the time of writing, both authors were professors at a College of Business; Nitse was a professor of Marketing, while Parker was Assistant Professor of Computer Science. These authors first defines each discipline: competitive intelligence systems gathers information for use in the decision making process, KM systems are often used to organize the knowledge, and library science provides the structure for the storage of published documents irrespective of whether it is in printed or electronic format.

The authors suggest that all of these disciplines are linked by Archive Theory. That is, the process by which an archive of information is built. Through this process the decision is made about what documents or information to retain and what format to use in retaining them.

Parker, K. R., Nitske, P. S., & Flowers, K. A. (2005). Libraries as knowledge management centers. *Library Management, 26*(4-5), 176-189.

In this paper the authors propose a new service for libraries, one that will assist small businesses in competing more effectively with larger competitors. The authors propose enhancing libraries to act as knowledge management (KM) centers for small businesses, providing both KM and competitive intelligence (CI) services. The requirements for a Library Knowledge Management Center (LKMC) are presented and briefly examined. KM, CI, ontologies, and the semantic web are all considered, and the steps needed to realize a LKMC are presented. The authors also provide an approach to developing an LKMC as well as a rationale for the proposal. Finally, they address future research issues for realization of their proposal.

From a practical perspective, this article is useful because if this proposal is followed up with future research, it will prove beneficial to both small business and to libraries. Small businesses are not always able to gather sufficient internal and external knowledge to assist in strategic planning and positioning, and thus are unable to compete with larger rivals whose resources allow them to develop sophisticated KM and CI systems. LKMCs hold promise to level the playing field. Libraries will benefit because this proposal will reaffirm their relevance in a digital age in which so much information is freely available to patrons.

Owen, J.M.(1999). Knowledge management and the information professional. *Information Services and Use, 19*(1), 7-16.

In this article, the author posits that while information management and knowledge management (KM) are quite distinct concepts, information management can fulfill an important role within the broader concept of KM. He argues that KM is an extremely broad concept, involving almost any area and issue in the organization. As a result, the perception of the individual is based on the role they play in the organization. From the author's perspective, librarians' knowledge is managed by means of storage and retrieval systems, distribution networks, etc. This he feels, is a fairly modest role in view of the wider implications of the concept of KM. In order for KM to be successful the author states, there must be the support and commitment of top management. If the information professional keeps that in mind, and happens to have a responsive senior management that understands its responsibilities, then the librarian or information professional will find exciting opportunities to contribute to the new domain of KM.

42

Pantry, S. & Griffiths, P. (2003). Librarians or knowledge managers: What's in a name, or is there a real difference. *Business Information Review, 20*(2), 102-109. doi: 10.1177/0266382103202011.

The authors in this article point out that in recent years some libraries have changed their names to information or knowledge centers, and librarians have begun to be called by other names, such as knowledge managers. They observe that there is a tendency for these new titles and functions to be very poorly defined and the qualities needed to do the job are frequently not known or understood by potential employers. To reduce this confusion, producers and users of information services must take a wide variety of issues into consideration, including: the cost of information; whether it is priced or free; accessibility, whether the information is in the right place at the right time; the skills necessary to access information and use it efficiently; quality and timeliness; and the most cost-effective ways to produce and use information and the most intuitive ways of presenting it.

The authors conclude that many skills are common to both librarians and knowledge managers. Both select, collect and disseminate information, link it to the users and train those users to use information efficiently and effectively. Both operate in the context of the organization or community that they serve. What may ultimately prove more important than any difference between them is the quality of their skills and the alliances they forge with other players such as the managers of the business's technology and the most important users of the information service. Viewed in this light, the authors conclude that there is no difference between the skills of a librarian and that of a knowledge manager.

Perez, E. (1999). Knowledge management in the library–not. *Database Magazine,* 22(2), 75-78.

The author in this article discusses the lack of involvement of librarians and corporate libraries in the knowledge management (KM) activities of their organizations, and considers this a very unfortunate circumstance. He maintains that most of the time significant KM projects are assigned to the information systems or information technology staff, rather than to librarians. He argues that even though librarians have excellent skills in storing and retrieving facts, images, documents, books and articles, they lack skills in the requisite self-promotion work of aggressively capitalizing on their accomplishments. The author examines some approaches that librarians can take to familiarize themselves with the fundamental principles of KM and to study models for productive library information system applications. He provides two examples of library KM applications: *Refquest* at the Ithaca College Library, and *Information Dispatch* at the Multnomah County Public Library. He considers the possibilities of library information KM, and concludes that library science can benefit tremendously by applying KM methods and technology.

Porumbeanu, O. (2009). Strategic model for implementing *knowledge management* in *libraries* and information services. *Library & Information Science Research,* 13, 89-105.

In this article the author presents a strategic model for implementing knowledge management (KM) in libraries and information services. This model is created on the basis of the results from theoretical researches and practical applications in organizations from different countries and different fields of activity. The research also takes into account the specific characteristics of libraries and information services. The author points out that in most fields of activity there is an obvious trend towards both knowledge-based organizations and flexible organizations that encourage innovation and change. In this context, however, KM has become a fundamental process for all types of organizations in society. Libraries and information services are an integral part of the knowledge system and as a result, contribute to knowledge development.

This article is interesting because the author goes into great detail of the model which is based on five fundamental elements from which one should begin implementation of a KM function in the organizations engaged in information transfer.

Ralph, L., & Tijerino, C. (2009). Knowledge management and library culture. *College and Undergraduate Libraries, 16*(4), 329-337. doi: 10.1080/10691310903355960.

In this paper, the authors acknowledge the importance of knowledge management (KM), or the effective use of knowledge, and recognize that KM has been practiced successfully by many organizations. Although KM began with businesses, the authors point out that individual libraries and librarians have periodically utilized KM. However, on a comprehensive scale, the library culture seems divided. In this paper the authors examine the attitudes and practices of two distinct groups of specialized librarians and their relationship to the use of KM tools. The research reveals that while one group of librarians embraces and assiduously utilizes KM, another group refrains from using KM even when an appropriate tool is available.

Ralph, L. (2009). If you build it they may not come: The case of QuestionPoint. *Electronic Journal of Academic and Special Librarianship, 10*(2).

In this article, the author questions whether a knowledge management (KM) tool that is readily accessible would be used by reference librarians. The Knowledge Base (KB) of QuestionPoint (QP) can be described as a KM tool because it is capable of capturing the collective knowledge of reference librarians for future use. In this research, the author answers the question by utilizing descriptive research as the methodology. She also used an unobtrusive study, a survey instrument, and interviews. Based on the findings, the author concludes that despite the technological capabilities of this KB, librarians who had access to the system failed to utilize it.

Ralph, L., & Ellis, T. (2009). An investigation of knowledge management solution for the improvement of reference services. *Journal of Information, Information Technology, and Organizations, 4.* 17-38.

In this study the authors investigate the use of the knowledge base of QuestionPoint as a knowledge management (KM) tool capable of improving reference services in academic libraries. The research addresses the problem that reference librarians continually provide ineffective service to patrons. Because of the expansive exposure to resources, it is often difficult for any individual librarian to accurately recall the best resource or answer for any specific question. While individual librarians may not recall specific information, when they collaborate with their colleagues and share their collective knowledge there is usually an improvement in the quality of service they provide. It would benefit librarians therefore, if they use a knowledge management tool that could capture and store their communal knowledge for future use.

This study explores the librarians' perceptions of the benefits and problems of using the knowledge base and the impact of the knowledge base in reducing response time and duplication. This descriptive research entailed: an unobtrusive study of reference librarians at libraries that had purchased the KB, and a survey/interview of those reference librarians to gauge their attitudes toward the KB. The study reveals that the reference librarians did not generally use the KB, one of the classic causes of failure in a KM implementation. As a result there was duplication of effort and no reduction in response time.

Reardon, D.F. (1998). *Knowledge management: The discipline for information and library science professionals*. Paper presented to the 64th annual IFLA conference, Amsterdam.

In this paper the author examines and responds to an assertion that librarians are knowledge managers. According to Reardon, the view expressed in the literature is that knowledge management (KM) is a rapidly developing area that has its roots in the recent past; and that interest in it has increased somewhat meteorically mainly because of the revolutionary rather than evolutionary changes that are occurring in the business and public sectors internationally. Reardon observes that researchers suggest that KM is an emerging discipline within information and library science and that elements useful to KM have been present in syllabi for some long time. These researchers, according to Reardon, also make suggestions as to what should be included in the content of "real" KM courses developed for Schools of Library and Information Science.

Reczek, K. (2009). Ask a Librarian. *Computers in Libraries, 29*(6): 43.

Karen Reczek, senior manager at the Information Resources Center of the firm and author of this article focuses on the use of knowledge management (KM) tools by the library of Bureau Veritas Consumer Products Services Inc. She shares information on how her organization uses KM to promote innovation. According to Reczek, members of the library team share lessons learned and best practices on a daily basis. She also adds that the information center has developed several homegrown applications to capture, codify and disseminate knowledge, including their corporate intranet. This practice Reczek emphasizes, has facilitated the sharing of information in an effective manner.

Robb, B. G. (2009). KM in hospitals: Drawing from experience to define the librarian's role. *Journal of Hospital Librarianship, 9*(3): 307-317. doi: 10.1080/15323260903015681

This article is the result of a workshop in which the author participated. In the article the author shares her experiences working with information professionals from corporate and hospital environments. This workshop was to envision how the concepts of knowledge management (KM) and transfer—as applied in the corporate environment—could be applied in a hospital/health system. The workshop session used the process of Appreciative Inquiry to facilitate a positive conversation. Participants shared their experiences in knowledge transfer activities— both traditional and expansive in nature. Together they built a list of skill sets that librarians already embody to help organizations support their knowledge transfer efforts that may not have been recognized by leadership or the librarians themselves. The participants' positive experiences illustrated how these skills might enhance knowledge-sharing activities in hospitals. The group discussed how an expanded, proactive knowledge role could be implemented by hospital librarians. They drafted descriptions of Plan-Do-Study-Act projects to test the potential outcomes of this expanded application.

The author hypothesizes that an explicit role for hospital librarians in sustaining successful knowledge transfer could contribute to organizational learning about error and quality improvement. The work begun by this group aimed to launch future discussions and studies on the role of librarians in KM activities in hospitals. The author concludes that the future of hospital librarians is measured by how successful they are in adapting to new demands and in seeing innovative opportunities that have impact in the acute care setting.

Roknuzzaman, M., & Umemoto, K. (2009). How library practitioners view knowledge management in libraries: A qualitative study. *Library Management, 30*, (8-9), 643-656.

In this paper the author investigates the original views of library practitioners regarding knowledge management (KM) in libraries. The study is based on the review of literature available in secondary sources, and the result of interviews of ten library practitioners worldwide. The respondents were purposively selected from the participants of two international conferences held in 2008. The interviews were conducted through e-mail using a short, structured, and open-ended questionnaire. The research revealed that the degrees of understanding of KM concepts among the library practitioners are varied. Most library practitioners have focused on a shallow perception of KM for its incorporation into library practice - dealing with only explicit information and/or knowledge. This study also finds some of the reasons for being responsive to KM, e.g. increasing value of knowledge in the knowledge economy, role of information technologies, and opportunities for improved library practices.

The study is limited in its scope, because it conducted interviews of only ten library practitioners worldwide, and therefore the sample is not large enough to make any generalizations from the findings. Despite this inadequacy of the research however, the author suggests that library practitioners need to broaden their understanding, change their traditional mindset, and apply a holistic approach of KM system design and library practice, focusing on both explicit and tacit knowledge.

Rowley, J. (1999). What is knowledge management? *Library Management, 20*(8), 416.

In this article the author discusses the role of knowledge management (KM) and points out that KM does not only involve the organization of knowledge but more importantly requires changing the culture, the values and the ways of working within the organization. According to the author it is important to realize that the knowledge to be managed involved both the explicit documented knowledge and tacit embedded knowledge. Therefore it is important for all groups of information professionals to find a way to integrate these various competencies and skills to contribute to the knowledge base of their organization. This article is useful because it underscores the importance of KM in any organization. This author shares the view of Schwarzwalder (1999) that changing the culture is essential to the effective use of KM.

Ryan, F. (1998). The future of the librarian in knowledge management.
   Knowledge Management Review, 1(4): 6-8.

   In this article, the author discusses the role of corporate librarians
in knowledge management (KM) in the workplace. Ryan believes that the
corporate librarians are perfectly positioned to assume the leadership in
the adoption, development and maintenance of KM initiatives. Librarians,
the author feels are so intimately concerned with people and the sharing of
knowledge that they participate in KM activities effortlessly. As a result,
everyone in the organization would benefit with the librarian at the helm.
According to Ryan, corporate librarians have all the knowledge, tools and
contacts to design, develop and maintain the links between knowledge
workers and the external knowledge they need to support decision-making
and keep the knowledge for which they were hired current and accurate.
He observes that librarians are customer driven and their participation in
multi-disciplinary KM initiatives will greatly increase the probability of
success.

Ryder-Cox, J. A., Chavez, R. F., Smith, D. A., Mahoney, A., & Crane, G. R.
   (2000). Knowledge management in the Perseus Digital Library. *Ariadne,*
   25.

   In this paper the authors describe the new document delivery and
knowledge management tools utilized in the Perseus Digital Library.
According to the authors, digital libraries can be an extremely effective
method of extending the services of a traditional library because they
enable activities such as access to materials outside the physical confines
of the library. The true benefit of a digital library, however, comes not
from the replication and enhancement of traditional library functions, but

rather in the ability to make possible tasks that would not be possible outside the electronic environment. Such tasks includes the hyper textual linking of related texts, full text searching of holdings, and the integration of knowledge management, data visualization, and geographic information tools with the texts in the digital library. One of the challenges in building this type of system, the authors insist, is the ability to apply these sorts of tools in a scalable manner to a large number of documents tagged according to different levels of specificity, tagging conventions, and document type definitions (DTDs). To address this challenge, the authors explained how they developed a toolset to manage XML and SGML documents of varying DTDs for the Perseus Digital Library. This toolset is able to extract structural and descriptive metadata from documents, deliver well formed document fragments on demand to a text display system, and when combined with other modules support the sort of advanced applications required to effectively utilize a digital library.

Ryske, E. J., & Sebastian, T. B. (2000). From library to a knowledge center: The evolution of a technology infocenter. In K. Srikantaiah & M. Koenig. (Eds). *Knowledge Management for the Information Professional, (pp. 365-388).* Medford, NJ: Information Today.

In this chapter the authors conduct a case study and share the results of the successful evolution of a corporate library to a knowledge center, incorporating knowledge management (KM) initiatives. According to the authors, the transition revealed that mutual benefits are achieved when a special library teams up with KM initiatives in an organization. The case study demonstrates three main points: (1) the evolution from library to knowledge center provides value to both the internal customers and the information professionals of the InfoCenter, (2) The first step in the evolution is the subtle, but important shift in the way the InfoCenter defines its role and (3) a corporate library can benefit by teaming with other knowledge initiatives in the organization and those initiatives can benefit by teaming with the library.

Sarrafzadeh, M., Hazeri, A., & Martin, B. (2006). Knowledge management education for LIS professionals: Some recent perspectives. *Journal of Education for Library & Information Science, 47*(3), 218-237.

In this article the authors report the findings from an international survey investigating the implications of knowledge management (KM) for the library and information science (LIS) profession. The authors surveyed members of two international mailing lists and assessed the reasons for the inclusion of KM in library education. They also considered the view that the nature and content of KM programs needed to meet the challenges of the work environment. The findings reveal that there is a strong interest among LIS professionals toward the inclusion of KM in their educational programs. This inclusion provides the opportunity to expand the skills of LIS professionals and facilitate their entry into the KM job market. The authors believe that for most LIS professionals in this study, a curriculum which embodies core elements of LIS, management, and information systems would best meet the needs of LIS professionals in a KM work environment.

Schwarzwalder, R. (1999). Librarians as knowledge management agents. *EContent, 22*(4), 63-65.

In this article the author discusses his view of knowledge management (KM) and the role librarians could play in its implementation. According to the author, there is a clear distinction between information management and KM. Information management is the consistent and logical treatment of data so that people are able to retrieve resources. KM, however, is concerned with developing organizations in such a manner as to derive knowledge from information. The author states that in order to be successful in KM it was essential to establish a culture that promoted the sharing of information. KM should also operate in a manner that paid attention to the process of any project or workflow and captured this process through documentation and lessons learned and this knowledge should then be stored in a manner that facilitated future use.

The author, who, at the time of writing, was a librarian at Ford Motor Company, also discusses the role of the library in KM. According to the author while librarians may not influence change in the organizational culture, librarians are very effective in information sharing and they fully understand the ways in which people communicate information needs and their patterns of information use. This article is useful because it addresses the value of KM in libraries, and the role of librarians as the agents of KM.

Senapati, S.K. (2006). Knowledge management, library and literature. *SRELS Journal of Information Management, 43*(4): 333-340.

In this paper the author provides an overview of knowledge, knowledge management (KM) and libraries. The author discusses different aspects of KM in a library and clarifies the basics of knowledge managers and the role of librarians. The author also enumerates the seminars and conferences held during the last five years at the national and international level on KM. He points out that these conferences contributed to the enhancement of the literature pertaining to KM, library and literature.

Shanhong, T. (2000, August). *Knowledge management in libraries in the 21st century*. Paper presented at the 66th Annual IFLA Council and General Conference held in Jerusalem, Israel.

In this paper the author discusses the knowledge economy, its sub-discipline, knowledge management (KM), and its relevance to libraries in the 21st century. According to the author, the knowledge economy is a new concept that has appeared worldwide in recent years. As a sub-discipline of the knowledge economy, KM is a completely new concept and method of management. KM, the author posits, works for converting the intellectual assets of workers and staff members in the organization into higher productive forces - competition power and new value. KM requires linkage of information with information, information with activities, and information with man - so as to realize the sharing of knowledge (including tacit and explicit knowledge). The conventional functions of a library are to collect, process, disseminate, store, and utilize document information to provide service for the society. In the knowledge economy era, the library becomes a treasure-house of human knowledge, participates in knowledge innovation, and becomes an important link in the knowledge innovation chain. The author firmly believes that in the 21st century, the library will inevitably face and utilize KM.

Skyrme, D. (1997, December). *From information management to knowledge management: Are you prepared?* Paper presented at the Online Information International Conference, London, England.

In this paper the author has drawn together two main strands of current management focus - the Internet and knowledge management. Each has a momentum of its own. However, in combination, they provide a powerful driving force for business and individual opportunities. The author summarizes some highlights from the research into this interaction and indicates some of the ways in which information professionals and online service providers can exploit this convergence.

The author concludes that collaborative technologies and information management both have significant contributions to make, but that many organizations have yet to adopt them both systematically and strategically. Implications are developed for online service providers and information professionals in how they might achieve their full potential in moving forward the strategic knowledge agenda.

The knowledge agenda and the growth of the Internet means that there is an opportunity to elevate the skills developed over many years in handling information to a higher level and become active in the knowledge agenda. Undoubtedly the overall visibility of information professionals needs to be improved. On the one hand, the Internet makes information more readily accessible to the end-user, thus to some extent by passing the need to get involved in mundane activities. On the other hand, it has created a heightened awareness of what information is available, yet tools, such as search engines, may not be effectively used.

Skyrme, D. (2004). *Information managers do we need them?* Paper presented at the Online Information International Conference Proceedings, December 2004, 149-155.

This paper represents a follow-up paper presented by this author at the Online Conference in December 1997. In this paper the author analyzes key developments and trends in information and knowledge management (KM), and discusses how they impact the future role of information professionals. According to the author, the provision of information has recently improved significantly. As a result, there are increasing problems of information overload and timely, accurate retrieval. This raises not only questions about the effectiveness of information management and information professionals, but also, given the significant advances in technology, whether information professionals are even necessary.

Snyman, R. M. M. (2001). Do employers really know what they want? An analysis of job advertisements for information and knowledge managers. *Aslib Proceedings, 53*(7), 273-281. doi: 10.1108/EUM0000000007061.

In this article the author reports on the findings and analysis of what organizations communicate to the outside world regarding their needs for information and knowledge managers. To conduct the study, the author examined information about employment opportunities and requirements for the position of information and knowledge managers from job advertisements which appeared in the three weekly national newspapers with the highest circulation figures. If this study is used as a gauge of how organizations manage or intend to manage information and knowledge, it appears that an awareness of effective information and knowledge management (KM) in organizations exists, although a comprehensive understanding of the field is lacking and should be improved. The author believes that organizations should be aware of the fact that what they communicate to the public via job advertisements indicates their insight into the knowledge of the subject. The findings reveal that employers seem to have a problem in defining the position and role of the information and knowledge manager in their organizations.

Southon, G., & Todd, R. (1999). Knowledge management: Education for the knowledge age. Education for library and information services. *Australia (ELIS: A), 16*(3), 21-30.

In this article, the authors discuss knowledge management (KM) as it pertains to education for library and information services. They describe the establishment of a Graduate Diploma in Knowledge Management in the Department of Information Studies at the University of Technology in Sydney, Australia. This diploma was developed for the purpose of assisting in producing information professionals with the additional skills and knowledge required to move into this very dynamic career area. The authors explore the development of the concept of KM by discussing the literature that has been contributed to it.

According to Southon and Todd, this study is relevant because the dramatic changes taking place in the commercial arena present opportunities and challenges for information professionals to expand their horizons and use their special skills in the management of information, thus becoming key contributors to the development of KM. The authors recognize the difficulty of defining the topic and the role to be played in it by information professionals.

Southon, G. & Todd, R. (2001). Library and information professionals and knowledge management: Conceptions, challenges and conflicts. *The Australian Library Journal, 50*(3), 259-281.

The authors of this article discuss a study conducted to identify the perceptions, challenges and conflicts of knowledge management (KM) as perceived by library and information science professionals in Australia. Fifty-six library and information professionals participated in the study. The authors used both a questionnaire and two focus groups to gather their data. The findings reveal that there are various perceptions of KM. For example, some participants are of the opinion that KM is faddish and likely to disappear or change form. Others believe that librarians need to take KM seriously because it could significantly enhance their role. Various suggestions are made on how to recognize the importance of KM in the information science field. The study provides little evidence that KM activities are situated within the broader mission and objectives of the organization, linked to organizational goals, and mainstreamed into the wider culture and practices of the organization. Finally, the study reveals that there are so many varied approaches and perceptions of KM that it is difficult to identify much commonality.

Stern, D. (2003). New knowledge management systems: The implications for data discovery, collection development, and the changing role of the librarian. *Journal of the American Society for Information Science, 54*(12), 1138-1140.

This article is part of a series of papers presented at the 2002 Tri-Society Symposium on Chemical Information and it highlighted questions that should be considered as new paradigms for information storage and retrieval systems are developed. The author discusses the role of the librarian in this environment. According to the author, the role of the librarian is no longer to simply purchase and implement the latest commercial tools and train users in new research techniques. Instead, the librarian is now responsible for influencing the future by reviewing and revising current tools and collaborating on, "the design of scalables, integrated extensive components of the information network" (p. 1140).

Additionally the author, a librarian, states that librarians must educate the population and they should also teach critical thinking skills as well as how to perform a variety of search techniques. They should also become intimately involved in the long-term viability of the entire infrastructure of the system. This article is useful because it provides a general overview of the need for new KM systems and the new role of librarians.

60

Stoker, D. (1999). Wanted-an innovative and visionary evidence
based/knowledge management librarian. *Journal of Librarianship and
Information Science, 31*(2): 67-69.

In this article the author examines the range of job titles for information professionals which appear in job advertisements, and notes the current return to popularity of the terms ``library'' and ``librarian'' after many years in retreat. The author conducted an analysis of job advertisements which reveals five factors that have brought about the various changes in library and information terminology: (1) professionalization of modern library and information practice; (2) growth in the range and complexity of educational qualifications, with associated competition among institutions; (3) impact of other disciplines or professions; (4) developments in information technology; and (5) the developing role of information within society. Stoker expands upon these factors, and weighs their relative importance in driving the perceived changes in the profession.

Stover, M. (2004). Making tacit knowledge explicit: The ready reference database as codified knowledge. *Reference Services Review, 32*(2), 164-173.

In this article the author examines how an organization transformed the process of knowledge from tacit to explicit to codified. He then used the experience of San Diego State University and describes their web-based ready reference database and its conversion process in reference services. The author is a Psychology and Behavioral Sciences librarian in an academic library and well qualified to write on the topic.

This article is useful because it acknowledges the need for shared knowledge. To underscore the importance of knowledge sharing, he posed the question "How does a reference librarian with little knowledge in a particular field answer reference questions from that discipline" (p.164). Stover also recognizes the need to establish a tool to manage knowledge and describes how having such a tool enhances the effectiveness of reference service.

Sutton, M. (2007). Examination of the historical sense-making processes representing the development of knowledge management programs in universities: Case studies associated with an emergent discipline. (Doctoral Dissertation). Retrieved from *Dissertation Abstracts* (AAT NR32329).

The purpose of this qualitative study is to investigate the phenomenon of Knowledge Management (KM) program design and development. The interest in KM programs has grown during the last decade because of the increased demand for KM educational research and the importance of the emerging knowledge economy. The author in this exploratory and explanatory investigation scrutinized two cases of graduate KM programs conceived in the year 2000.

The findings reveal the struggles amongst diverse educational program stakeholders. The teams responded to the challenges of ambiguous frameworks, contradictory opinions from experts, inconsistent definitions, and untested learning outcomes. The results include a valuable repository of provisional Bodies of Knowledge, courses, definitions, frameworks, learning outcomes, and position profiles. The major conclusions are that: (1) the programs are triggered by the need for generating new revenue streams at the educational institutions: (2) deep knowledge about KM is not necessary in order to design and develop an

educational program; (3) the two institutions established KM programs
because of passionate leaders and teams, group and personal agility and
self-learning, innovative and creative curricula; (4) librarians and
information professionals play a pivotal role in conceiving, designing, and
developing the programs; and (5) KM does not exhibit the characteristics
of a mature field with the experiences represented by these two cases.

The article is interesting because it reveals new, previously
unknown knowledge about the inner workings of KM educational
program design and development. Leaders of schools of Business, Library
and Information Science (LIS), and Management could benefit
significantly from the results if they wish to reduce the "time and cost to
market" of a KM program. Increased involvement by LIS faculty could
boost the relevance and relationship of the LIS field to KM education.

Teng, S. (2002). Knowledge management in public libraries. *ASLIB Proceedings,
54(3)*, 188-197.

In this article the author investigates the current knowledge
management (KM) practices of the Singapore National Library Board
(NLB). He demonstrates how KM can effectively be applied to the NLB
to tie in with its mission statement of expanding the learning capacity of
the nation, of enhancing the nation's competitiveness, and of promoting a
gracious society. While KM as a business concept has been traditionally
applied to money-making organizations with the goal of enhancing and
improving operations to gain competitive advantage and increase profits,
KM can also be applied to nonprofit organizations such as government
bodies and statutory boards. According to Teng, KM can also be used to
improve communication among staff and between top management, and it

helps to instill a culture of sharing and to promote and implement a performance-based reward system for employees. The author insists that KM involves a complex process of aligning the company's mission statement with the best practices that enable the company to be competitive and profitable in its sector.

Townley, C.T. (2001). Knowledge management and academic libraries. *College and Research Libraries, 62*(1), 44.

In this article the author examines the benefits of knowledge management (KM) to improve the effectiveness of academic libraries in the United States. Townley observes that KM is a new field that draws on several disciplines including library and information science. He points out that although KM was developed in corporate America, it is beginning to reach public service and educational institutions. He asserts that KM can improve effectiveness in libraries if incorporated into many of its operations, because it offers the opportunity to expand the role of libraries in the academic community. If implemented successfully, Townley believes, KM could strengthen relationships both internal and external relationships of the university. Finally, Townley insists that KM is a social phenomenon which is both similar to and different from academic libraries; thus librarians and knowledge workers must resolve any differences before they can work together effectively.

Turvey, M. R., & Letarte, K. M. (2002). Cataloging or knowledge management: Perspectives of library educators on cataloging education for entry-level academic librarians. *Cataloging & Classification Quarterly, 34*(1/2), 165-187.

In this article the authors report the results of a study which explores the views of library educators with regard to cataloging education. Participating in this study were 23 educators with primary teaching duties in reference, 29 educators with primary teaching duties in cataloging, and 70 educators whose primary teaching duties were in neither reference nor cataloging. All of these educators were from ALA-accredited master's degree programs and responded to a survey based on the Association for Library Collections and Technical Services (ALCTS) Education Policy Statement. The findings reveal that entry-level academic librarians will face a number of challenges as the catalog evolves from Online Public Access Catalog (OPAC) to information service. The number of re- sources available to users, particularly digital resources, continues to proliferate. As the responsibility for resource description becomes more widely distributed, an understanding of the fundamental principles of cataloging as well as the broader areas of knowledge management (KM) and information organization is essential for academic librarians working in all areas of the field.

This study is important because it confirms the importance of cataloging competencies for all entry-level academic librarians as perceived by library practitioners and library educators. Agreement between practitioners and library educators is crucial if graduates are to have the tools to overcome the challenges facing the profession. A dialogue between practitioners and library educators is vital not only to promote a set of core professional competencies, but also to pave the way for the continuing education that will fuel the success of the profession.

Van Rooi, H., & Snyman, R. (2006). A content analysis of literatures regarding KM opportunities for librarians. *ASLIB Proceedings, 58*(3), 261-271.

The purpose of this paper is to report on the progress of research regarding the opportunities for librarians within the context of knowledge management (KM). A content analysis of 28 full-length journal articles indexed by *Library Literature* in the past ten years was conducted. Findings indicate that more researchers than practitioners are aware of KM opportunities, utilize more literature reviews and base their findings on theory. In addition, an unexpected finding is that the majority of researchers communicate their results in professional rather than scholarly journals. Practitioners should therefore give attention to studies conducted by researchers to become aware of opportunities they could not identify themselves.

The authors admit the research had certain limitations; for example, only full-length journal articles indexed by *Library Literature* were included. Thus, the findings may have limitations in their generalizability. The authors believe however, that the results of the study may assist in the improvement of teaching and research in library and information science. Additionally, librarians may become aware of the opportunities and acquire guidelines on how to attain the necessary requirements towards enhancing their role and ultimately boosting their image. This study is useful because it demonstrates the progress of research regarding the KM opportunities for librarians, to researchers, and practitioners interested in this field.

Vitiello, G. (2009). Seven years after the open access revolution: (Research) Libraries as media and knowledge management centres. *Bollettino AIB, 49*(2), 171-179.

The author of this article focuses on the functionality of libraries as information centers in the midst of the availability of open access. Conducting a study after the existence of open access for seven years, findings reveal that open access makes information easily accessible on websites. Libraries, on the other hand, serve as knowledge management (KM) centers for open access publishing by soliciting from authors, establishing copyrights, and processing materials to conform to protocols.

Wagner-Dobler, R. (2004). Tacit knowledge, knowledge management, library science – No bridge between? *IFLA Publications, 108*, 39-46.

In this article, the author questions the relationship between knowledge management (KM) and library science, and ponders if there is a bridge that connects the two disciplines. The author reports on his review of the literature resulting from a discussion of scholars from various disciplines. During the discussion, the questions focused on the following: do libraries and library science really have an authentic bonding relationship with KM; is it legitimate in such a situation to christen libraries or documentation department centers of knowledge organization or even centers of KM, as happens now more and more; and is it sensible and possible for librarians and libraries, at least in firms, to even jump to the head of knowledge management movements in a situation where libraries or information services are not even mentioned in most of the literature on KM? The author observes that when the literature of KM is considered, there is a paucity of material that focuses on both library science and KM.

Webster, M. (2007). The role of library in knowledge management. In *Knowledge management: Social, cultural and theoretical perspectives,* edited by R. Rikowski. Oxford: Chandos Publishing.

In this chapter the author considers the transferability of the librarian or information professional's skills in knowledge management (KM). She focuses on a number of key areas, including database selection and management, focusing, in particular on library management systems; classification and taxonomies, current awareness, management training and information literacy, intranets and extranets, auditing needs, and market research and competitive intelligence. She believes that the need to manage lies at the heart of all KM initiatives and KM can be that transition from managing information to managing the library to managing the organization. Webster also believes that the biggest challenge for librarians is moving from managing explicit knowledge to facilitating and enabling the capture of tacit knowledge. She concludes by saying that for librarians and information professionals, there are "exceptional opportunities to become partners in creating and using knowledge not just providing a home for it and managing that home" (p. 91).

Wheaton, K. (2009). Making the transformation to sharing knowledge. *Information Outlook, 13*(6), 20-24.

In this article the author focuses on the concept of transforming the corporate library to become an entity that ensures it promotes knowledge sharing throughout the organization. Wheaton suggests that the librarians must ensure that library is always aligned with the vision and mission of the company. He adds that librarians must identify opportunities for library employees to encourage knowledge sharing within the organization. He observes that knowledge sharing is the most effective way to participate in knowledge management (KM). Thus he asserts that knowledge sharing could be best achieved if the appropriate people and process are in agreement. Only then should anyone implement a KM program and its accompanying technologies.

White, T. (2004, August). *Knowledge management in an academic library: A case study on knowledge management (KM) within Oxford University Library Services (OULS).* Paper presented at the World Library and Information Congress: 70th IFLA General Conference and Council in Buenos Aires, Argentina.

The author of this case study endeavors to examine a complex knowledge management (KM) concept through a practical approach in the knowledge environment. In this paper the author attempts to distinguish information from knowledge and define KM. He focuses on the KM elements in the academic environment with particular reference to the Oxford University Library Services (OULS) and outlines the need to include KM in library strategy in order to retain "Know-How' for the benefits of its staff and users. He discusses the tools and techniques for KM implementation and provides an analysis of the risks and benefits of the implementation of KM. This article is useful because it offers tools and techniques for KM implementation and provides a list of pros and cons.

Wormell, I. (2004). Skills and competencies required to work with knowledge management. *IFLA Publications, 108*, 107-114.

In this article the author discusses the skills and competencies required to work with knowledge management (KM). The author shares the view of established KM experts Davenport and Prusak that the awareness and application of knowledge have always been at the centre of the librarians' work, therefore, it is important that companies exploit the skills of people with librarianship and information backgrounds. Wormell points out that Davenport and Prusak also state that librarians need to change some things about how they do their work.

In this paper, the author points to some of the key issues supporting this viewpoint, and discusses the required new competence areas, which librarians have to adopt in their work. She also emphasizes that KM - idea of the moment - is a part of that range of skills, which entrepreneurial library and information professionals generally have. Librarians can be successful in KM if they take a wider view of their professional interest within their organization and use their skills to address not only information (particularly printed information) but knowledge, including who knows what, who knows whom, and where the knowledge resides. Thus, the author insists, if librarians learn to promote themselves and their achievements at every level, and start to act as if their role mattered, only then are they prepared to be actors in the knowledge transfer processes.

Zauha, J. (2003). Library intranets as knowledge management tools: Box of tricks or box of junk? *PNLA Quarterly, 68*(1), 9-11.

This article discusses the library's intranet as one of the knowledge management (KM) tools that libraries use. The author describes the intranet as an internal website and observes that while it could be beneficial, it could also be problematic. The author believes that the intranet could be very informative and a useful KM tool if well organized. However, if it is poorly organized, then it would not contribute to effective sharing of information. He offers suggestions for effective use and identifies potential problems and pitfalls.

The author, who is a reference team leader for a university and has been a member of her library's web team for several years, is well equipped to discuss this topic. The article is useful because it acknowledges the suite of KM tools in libraries then identifies one tool and demonstrates its strengths and suggests ways to avoid any potential pitfalls.

Electronic Resources

Charles, S. K. (2001). *Lessons from the document management trenches.*
Retrieved from
http://www.hpl.hp.com/techreports/2001/HPL-2001-230.pdf

In this case study, Charles (2001) examines Kalliope, the knowledge management (KM) project developed by librarians at Hewlett-Packard (HP). Although this was a project designed to serve everyone within the organization, the librarian was asked to spearhead the project because it was perceived that she had the requisite skills. At the time of writing, she was an information professional with experience as a technical researcher, "former cataloger, administrator for the online system, and webmaster," and these qualifications "seemed custom tailored to just such an undertaking" (p.1).

The project was undertaken because HP owned over four laboratories with information scattered among them. No one had access to all the information. Many documents had been created and stored on different lab servers and individual computers. As a result, there was no comprehensive way to locate or share the information. This resulted in the provision of poor customer service. HP decided to develop a knowledge system that all personnel could use to access, create, and store information in order to increase knowledge sharing, collaboration, and communication. This article is useful because it emphasizes the need for KM in libraries and the role the librarian could play in aiding the design of a comprehensive system to access or share information.

De Jager, M. (1999, April). *The KMAT: Benchmarking knowledge management*. Paper   presented at the conference. Retrieved from http://0-vnweb.hwwilsonweb.com.novacat.nova.edu/hww/results/resu.

In this article the author discusses knowledge management (KM) and emphasizes the need to share information. She offers the knowledge management assessment tool (KMAT) a KM tool developed by Arthur Andersen as a benchmarking instrument that could direct institutions towards areas that require more attention and identify KM practices in which they excel. The author discusses the benefits of sharing information and offers suggestions on how to encourage staff to willingly share information. She recommends making knowledge sharing part of the performance review criteria and suggests rewarding employees according to the quality and quantity of information they contribute to the KM system. This article is useful because it offers a background to KM and emphasizes the importance and relevance of KM to knowledge sharing.

Ferguson, S. (2009, Month, date). Information literacy and its relationship to knowledge management. *Journal of Information Literacy, 3*(2). Retrieved from http://ojs.ac.uk/ojs/index.php/JIL/article/view/PRA-v3-12-2009-1.

In this paper, the author explores the relationship between Information Literacy (IL) and knowledge management (KM). He approaches this exploration from three perspectives. First, he examines the perspective that library and information Science (LIS) professionals have a significant role to play in the KM environment, a role considerably strengthened by the profession's expertise in IL instruction. Secondly he examines the belief that IL and the fostering of an information literate workforce are key components in any KM initiative; and thirdly, he examines the LIS profession's long standing interest and expertise in IL instruction. The author argues that research in each domain can inform the other but because IL represents a fraction of the KM domain any attempts to do so may cause confusion rather than provide a pathway for information professionals and others pursuing workplace IL.This paper is useful because it provides recommendations for further research and suggests a scalar approach to conceptualizing KM and IL practice.

Ferguson, S., Sarrafzadeh, M., & Hazeri, A. (2007, April 29). Migrating LIS professionals into knowledge management roles: What are the major barriers? In Proceedings of Educause Australasia, Melbourne, Australia, April 29 -May 2, 2007 [Online]. Available http://www.caudit.edu.au/educauseaustralasia07/ authors_papers/sarrafzadel-114.pdf

Knowledge management (KM) the authors suggest, is a multi-dimensional field of study and practice, which requires a wide range of capabilities amongst its contributors, who come from a variety of professional groups. The author of this paper suggests that the Library and Information Services (LIS) profession should and indeed, is making a significant contribution to organizational KM. They outline KM knowledge and skills and review the major barriers to LIS engagement in KM: the profession's focus on external information resources, as distinct from internal organizational knowledge assets; lack of business knowledge; content ignorance; an image problem; a name problem; lack of visibility in the corporate environment; personality issues; and relative lack of the required management skills. The paper concludes with some suggested directions for LIS practitioners, educators and researchers.

Hart, N. (2006). Libraries aren't about books: Libraries are about people. Retrieved from http://smr-knowledge.com/wp-content/uploads/2010/01/ e-Profile_06-15- 06_Hart.pdf

In this article the author shares her point of view on the importance of knowledge management (KM) in libraries. She observes that in any organization, the main function of libraries is to support the research process. However, she asserts that while libraries have, and should continue to pay close attention to its collections and resources, it is equally important to focus on the people who require the services and the people who provide them. Hart, who is the Director of Knowledge and Information Services, believes that the approach of collaboration, working with people and identifying the best solutions for them is an effective way to utilize KM to provide enhanced services for library clientele. She admits that while her library practices these skills, it was not always easy. Over time however, it became easier and since its consistent use, productivity has increased, there is minimal staff turnover, and library patrons are happier.

Hart points out that there is great worth in the knowledge acquired in the organization through its people, and this knowledge, if managed effectively, could only enhance the value of the organization. She specifically stresses the importance of recognizing the significance of "mature workers." These workers she insists contribute to knowledge retention and therefore should be encouraged to return to the workplace and serve as mentors or coaches to the more junior, inexperienced employee.

Maponya, P.M. (2004). *Knowledge management practices in academic libraries: A case study of the University of Natal, Pietermaritzburg Libraries.* Retrieved from: http://mapule276883.pbworks.com/f/ Knowledge+management+practices+in+academic+libraries.pdf.

This is a report of the results of a case study conducted to establish the ways in which the academic librarians of the University of Natal, Pietermaritzburg Libraries could add value to their services by engaging in knowledge management (KM). Acknowledging that KM is a viable means by which academic libraries could improve their services in the present knowledge era, the author points out that evolving information and knowledge has impacted all organizations, including academic libraries, resulting in the enhanced importance of KM.

According to the author, the conventional function of academic libraries is to collect, process, disseminate, store, and utilize information to provide service to the university community. However, the environment in which academic libraries operate today is changing. Academic libraries are part of the university and its organizational culture. As a result, the role of academic libraries is changing to provide a competitive advantage for the parent universities. The success of academic libraries depends on their ability to utilize information and knowledge of its staff to better serve the needs of the academic community. This requires academic librarians to reappraise their functions, expand their roles and responsibilities to effectively contribute and meet the needs of a large and diverse university community.

Subramanian, N. (2007). Knowledge and information management in libraries: A new challenge for the library and information professionals in the digital environment.
Retrieved from http://library.igcar.gov.in/readit2007/conpro/s1/S1_5.pdf

In this paper the author focuses on the concept of knowledge management (KM) and the role of library and information professionals in managing the knowledge and information in the digital environment. This paper also describes the development and use of Information and Communication Technologies (ICT) in the library and information centers, and also highlights the importance of library and information professionals in organizations performing duties such as knowledge creation, acquisition, preservation and sharing knowledge and information. In discussing the development of Information Technology (IT) and its applications in library and information centers, the author discusses the concept of document management that has been changed to information management, and again the entire scenario of information management that has started its change to KM.

Valera, J. (2004). From librarian to knowledge manager. *The Lawyer*. Retrieved from
http://units.sla.org/toronto/newsletter/courier/v36n2/v36n2a1.htm

In this article, the author states that the transformation from librarian to knowledge manager is inevitable and currently occurring. However, a deeper look at the direction that technology is taking, reveal the possibility of more far-reaching changes for organizations. To adjust to these changes, information professionals such as librarians must search beyond current bounds and think in terms of benefits to their organizations and the most effective way of sharing knowledge through information. Valera posits that if information is to be seamlessly integrated with transaction processes, then someone must scope out work-related behaviors to ensure that it is done in the most efficient and effective manner. And, if equal information and technology is available to everyone, then competition rests on the ability to interpret and apply these tools. The author concludes that the impending shift to knowledge management (KM) and beyond represents an exciting change for special librarians. However, it is an opportunity that requires a great deal of preparation, and a new way of thinking.

Wen, S. (2005). Implementing knowledge management in academic libraries: A pragmatic approach. Proceedings of the 3rd China-US Library Conference.
Retrieved from http://www.nlc.gov.cn/culc/en/index.htm.

In this paper the author suggests a pragmatic approach to the implementation of knowledge management (KM) for academic libraries utilizing the existing staffing, technology, and management structure. The author points out that KM is an emerging field, much touted or hyped since the late 1990s. However, due to the complicated nature of knowledge per se and its consequent management, it is often difficult to estimate or demonstrate the value of KM. As a result, academic libraries, with limited budget and human resources, may hesitate to follow the business sector and plunge into the uncharted sea of KM. Thus the author offers a practical approach to the successful implementation of KM.

Books

DuPlessis, M. (2006). *The impact of organizational culture on knowledge management for information professionals.* Oxford: Chandos Publishing.

This book is aimed at knowledge management (KM) professionals and students in the field of KM and information science. In this book the author highlights issues in organizational cultures that can impact the implementation of KM. Organizational culture has an extremely high impact on KM, but is very difficult to identify and to address. The book demonstrates how people, culture, technology, strategy, leadership, operational management, process and organizational structure issues all have an impact on the implementation of KM in any organization including libraries. The book also provides a model to identify and manage areas in the organization that impact KM. This mode is an easy and practical way to apply successful KM programs.

Hobohm, H. (Ed.) (2004). Knowledge management: Libraries and librarians taking up the challenge. *IFLA Publications, 108.*

This publication is a compilation of 17 papers given at various IFLA and some other conferences. A special knowledge management (KM) discussion group existed during these years and held meetings during the annual IFLA conferences. The papers are grouped into three sections: (1) Political and Ethical Implications; (2) Issues and Instruments and (3) Case Studies. In the papers in this volume, the authors discuss some of the fundamental implications of KM as an essential activity area for libraries. The authors also analyze key issues and instruments of KM and provide some examples of best practices.

Rikowski, R. (2007). (ed.). *Knowledge management: Social, cultural and theoretical perspectives.* Oxford: Chandos Publishing.

In this book the editor compiles a collection of essays from various authors who examine knowledge management (KM) from a number of different perspectives - social, philosophical, economic, cultural and theoretical. She includes contributions from a variety of KM experts and academics. In the essays, the authors consider a wide variety of issues, including KM and wisdom, KM and intangible value, web-based accessibility, KM and the library profession, KM and leadership, KM and cultural issues in both the developed and the developing world and even thermodynamics and KM. Some authors not only embrace this range of issues, but also raise a number of questions about the function and usefulness of the way knowledge is managed and disseminated. Consequently other authors provide an alternative view on KM, emphasizing that KM helps to ensure the continued success of the knowledge revolution.

Srikantaiah, T.K., & Koenig, M. (eds), ASIS. (2000). *Knowledge management for the information professional.* Medford, NJ: Information Today.

According to editors of this book, their primary concern in compiling this source is to teach knowledge management (KM) to graduate students in library and information science, business schools, records management, and related disciplines. In particular, the editors emphasize the social and cultural components of KM implementation. The book is organized into five sections: (1) "Overview of Knowledge Management," (2) "Background & Issues," (3) "Creating the Culture of Learning & Knowledge Sharing in the Organization," (4) "Knowledge Management Tools," and (5) "Knowledge Management Applications." The contributions are by 28 authors, the majority of whom are faculty members from schools of library and information science. Only two chapters deal specifically with libraries. These two chapters are, Chapter 5, "Is knowledge management really the future for information professionals?" written by Albert, and Chapter 10 "From library to a knowledge center: The evolution of a technology infocenter," written by Ryske and Sebastian.

This book is useful because it contains very interesting appendices. For example, Appendix A contains a copy of a course syllabus for a graduate course in a School of Library and Information Science and in a Graduate School of Business. Appendix B contains a bibliography of resources on *Knowledge management and the information professional.*

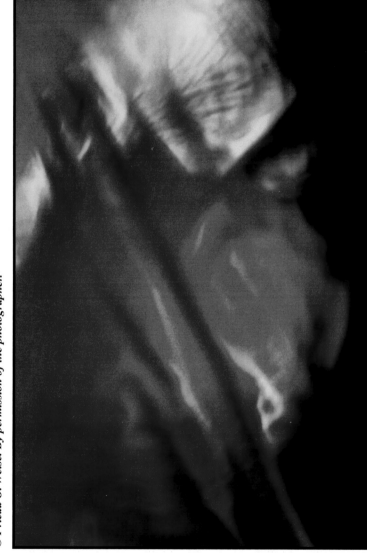

Abstract 1

AUTHOR INDEX

Lynette Lawrence Ralph

Dr. Lynette Lawrence Ralph is Assistant Director of the Sims Memorial Library at Southeastern Louisiana University in Hammond. Dr. Ralph received her Ph.D. in Information Science from Nova Southeastern University in Florida.